DRAGONS
YOUNG EXPLORER SERIES

BEADED AND
MONITOR LIZARDS...

ERIK D. STOOPS

Faulkner's Publishing Group

This book is dedicated to Beau Lewis for his outstanding contribution to and knowledge of these wonderful reptiles.

Library of Congress Catalog Card Number 97-60519.

COVER PHOTO: Water Monitor by Terry Odegaard
DESIGNED BY: Graphic Arts & Production Inc., Plover, WI

Faulkner's Publishing Group
200 Paw Paw Ave. #124
Benton Harbor, MI 49022

©1997 by Erik Daniel Stoops
Faulkner's ISBN 1-890475-04-1 Lib

Table of Contents

Chapter One

What are Beaded and Monitor Lizards?

Are Monitors and Beaded Lizards related to dinosaurs?

What do lizards die from?

Read on to answer these questions and more.

What is a Beaded Lizard?

The Beaded Lizard is made up of two species of large, ground-dwelling lizards. One of these species is the Gila Monster (Hila Monster) of southwestern United States. The other is the big Mexican Beaded Lizard. They live in Mexico and parts of Central America. According to scientists, they are closely related to the Monitor Lizard and should be placed in that family. What makes these lizards unique from all other species is that they are venomous and earless.

by Wai Lui

BABY DUMERILS MONITOR

What is a Monitor Lizard?

Some species of Monitor Lizards can reach a length of 12 feet long. They have snakelike habits, using their forked tongue to taste the air. They belong to the family Varanidae (Vara-na-da). There are about 30 species known to science. The Monitor family is known for their long neck and tail, and their muscular limbs. Monitors are called by different names in other countries. For example, in Africa they are called Leguaans and in Australia they are known as Goannas.

5

If I want to see Monitors or Beaded Lizards, where should I look?

The safest place to see a lizard is at a zoo. Many zoos have several kinds of species on display from all over the world. It is best not to catch lizards from the wild and keep them in your home. Try to leave them where they belong.

GREEN TREE MONITOR
▼

What do Monitors and Beaded Lizards die from?

Many lizards die from *viruses* and bacteria which they catch from other lizards. Lizards can catch colds and cough and sneeze like we do. They may die of stress due to being held in captivity. They can die from *parasites* that crawl on their body and some that live in their body. *Poachers* may often kill lizards for their skin or catch them to sell to people. This is not very fair to the lizards.

Are Monitors and Beaded Lizards related to dinosaurs?

According to *herpetologists* and *scientists* many species of reptiles, including lizards, were thought to be related to the dinosaur. This is still up for debate. *Paleontologists* have found that the dinosaurs were more closely related to birds.

6

by Bill LuBack's Reptiles

BEADED LIZARDS, MONITORS AND EARLESS MONITORS

▲ GILA MONSTER

Gila Monster:

The Gila Monster is found in southwestern United States. It has a pink body with black bands or spots and can reach a length of 2 feet. It will store food during the winter months in its tail. Their favorite food is quail eggs, but they will also eat small mammals. This is one of two species of venomous lizards found in the world.

Mexican Beaded Lizard:

The Mexican Beaded Lizard is much larger than the Gila Monster. It can reach lengths of almost 3 feet. They are found in Mexico and parts of Central America. Their coloration is chocolate brown with yellow and white stripes and spots. They feed on small mammals and eggs.

BLACK BEADED LIZARD ▶

by Terry Odegaard

Komodo Dragon:

The Komodo Dragon is the largest of the Monitor species and is found on the small Indonesian island of Komodo. They are an ***endangered*** species of lizard and may reach a length of 10 feet (3m) and weigh up to 200 lbs. (90kg). They feed on small animals.

ACCORDING TO SCIENTISTS, THE TOTAL POPULATION ▶ OF KOMODO DRAGONS IN THE WILD IS ROUGHLY ESTIMATED TO BE 2000 TO 5000, BASED ON A STUDY IN 1971.

Borneo Earless Monitor:

This rare lizard, which is found on the island of Borneo, lacks ear openings. They like to spend their time underground where they eat earthworms and other animals. Scientists are still studying the interesting habits of this rare lizard. They believe this lizard is not a Monitor Lizard but very closely related. Zoologists find this species interesting because they are survivors of the animal group that gave rise to the modern day snakes, though they are not a missing link between snakes and lizards.

by Jessie Cohen/National Zoological Park Smithsonian Institution.

Crocodile Monitor:

This is also known as New Guinea Long-Tailed Monitor. Scientists have found this species has grown up to 9 feet long which makes them the second largest species of lizard. They feed on small fish, mammals and crocodile eggs.

by Terry Christopher

CROCODILE ▶
MONITOR

9

Chapter Two

Where are Beaded and Monitor Lizards Found?

What types of climate do Beaded Lizards live in?

What types of region do Monitors live in?

Read on to answer these questions and more.

What types of region do Beaded Lizards live in?

The Gila Monster makes its home in southwestern United States deserts. They enjoy crawling around in rocky canyons and washes. The Mexican Beaded Lizard lurks in canyons in Mexico and parts of Central America. There is a subspecies of Beaded Lizard found in a remote area of the rain forest of Guatemala.

by Erik D. Stoops

▲ DESERT MONITOR

What types of climate do Beaded Lizards live in?

The Gila Monster lives in hot, dry climates. Beaded Lizards are found from deserts to hillsides to rain forests.

DESERT HABITAT ▶

by Terry Odegaard

What types of region do Monitors live in?

Out of the 30 species of Monitors, most live in rain forest habitats. Some species, such as the Desert Monitor, like their home hot and dry. Monitors are found in Australia, Southeast Asia and Africa. The Komodo Dragon lives on the island of Komodo in Indonesia.

11

What types of climate do Monitors live in?

The Black Tree Monitor makes its home in rain forests of New Guinea where the temperatures range from 89 degrees during the day to 60 degrees at night. The Bengal Monitor likes temperatures around 90 degrees.

Do Monitors swim?

Yes. Many species of Monitors are very good swimmers. The Mangrove Monitor feeds on fish. The Australian Mertans Monitors use streams to get away from their enemies.

◀ BENGAL MONITOR

by Terry Odegaard

12

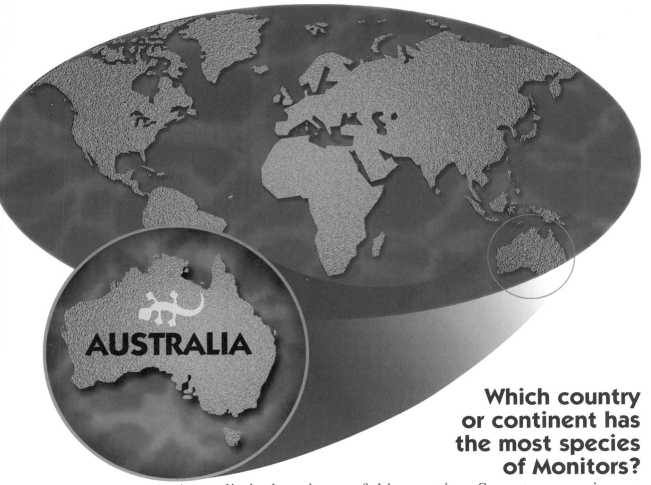

AUSTRALIA

Which country or continent has the most species of Monitors?

Australia is the winner of this question. Seventeen species are *endemic* to this continent alone. Other Monitor species are found in Asia, Africa, New Guinea and all islands of Indonesia. Can you find these places on the map above?

Chapter Three

Senses

What exactly do lizards see?

Do Monitors and Beaded Lizards have eyelids?

Read on to answer these questions and more.

Do Monitors and Beaded Lizards have tongues and what are they used for?

Lizards use their tongue for many different things. They use it to smell, taste and feel the vibrations in the air and on the ground, as well as to eat with.

Do Monitors and Beaded Lizards have eyelids?

Yes. Unlike snakes, all species of lizards have eyelids. Like our eyelids, they protect the lizard's eyes from dirt and predators.

What exactly do lizards see?

Lizards can see up close, but most species rely on their other senses to get them through the day and night.

by Terry Odegaard

▲
TEGU

Do Monitors and Beaded Lizards sleep?

Yes. Some species of Beaded Lizards and Monitors, such as the Desert Monitor, sleep all night. Others, like the Green Tree Monitor, sleep during the day and are active all night long during certain times of the year.

15

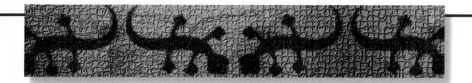

Chapter Four

Eating Habits

Depending on the species, lizards like to eat a variety of different plants and animals.

In this chapter you will find out what they like to eat, and how different prey help them live every day.

▲
ASIAN WATER MONITOR

by Erik D. Stoops

Do lizards eat other lizards?

Yes. Some species of lizards, such as the Ghould's Monitor feed on smaller lizards. The Water Monitor of Southeast Asia has been known to eat its own kind.

Do lizards eat dead things?

Some Monitor species feed on dead animals such as goats and rodents. The Komodo Dragon has been known to eat decaying pigs and will even dig up dead animals to eat.

What do Beaded Lizards eat?

Lizards eat many different things like mammals, reptiles, insects, fish and snails. Each species has its own type of food it eats. The Beaded Lizard likes to eat rodents. The Gila Monster likes to eat rodents and bird eggs.

17

Do lizards get fat?

In captivity, species that do not get very much exercise often become overweight. This is not healthy for lizards and can cause diseases.

How do lizards capture their food?

Lizards use their eyesight and their strong sense of smell to find food. Insect-eating Monitors may stay at a cricket nest and feed until all are full.

by Terry Odegaard

Do lizards chew their food?

No. They swallow their food whole. They use their teeth for tearing chunks and then swallow. Some lizards have very small teeth and use their tongue to help them eat. The Komodo Dragon is able to swallow large, oddly shaped pieces because its skull has moveable joints which allow the lizard's skull to enlarge in order to swallow its food.

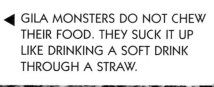

◀ GILA MONSTERS DO NOT CHEW THEIR FOOD. THEY SUCK IT UP LIKE DRINKING A SOFT DRINK THROUGH A STRAW.

▲
DUMERILS MONITOR

Do lizards store food in their tail?

Yes. Gila Monsters may store food in their tail all year-round. Their bodies use this food slowly. This helps them get through the winter months. Their tail can get very fat.

Do lizards have teeth?

Yes. Many species have teeth to grasp onto their food. Their teeth are also used to help them swallow food. The Komodo Dragon has very sharp teeth which helps it grab and tear its food.

Do lizards throw up?

When lizards get sick or have eaten something that doesn't agree with them, they often throw up. This is sometimes harmful to lizards because they tend to become dehydrated when this happens.

19

Chapter Five

Lizard Reproduction

Do Monitors and Beaded Lizards make good parents?

Will male lizards fight for the female?

Read on to answer these questions and more.

21

by Terry Odegaard

▲
THESE BABY LIZARDS ARE GETTING READY TO TAKE THEIR FIRST BREATH AND SEE THE WORLD FOR THE FIRST TIME.

Do Monitors and Beaded Lizards give live birth?

They give birth the same way as egg-laying species, through the anal plate. The **neonates**, "newborns," will often be born in an egg yolk placenta sack, which they usually break out of when born. Baby lizards use their egg tooth to do this. The egg tooth usually falls off in about a week. Sometimes the mother lizard will eat the placenta sacks. This provides nutrition for the exhausted mother lizards.

Do Monitors and Beaded Lizards make good parents?

No. Most species do not make good parents. After their young are born, the mother may never see the offspring again.

How many babies do Monitors and Beaded Lizards have?

Depending on the species, they have 2 to 30 babies at one time. A large Water Monitor may lay up to 30 eggs. All species of Monitors lay eggs which take anywhere from 79 to 181 days to hatch, depending on the species.

Will male lizards fight for the female?

Yes. Males will often court potential females and may often show signs of display to impress the female. In the Monitor species, males may often fight one another for the right to mate. The fight might look bad, but it is usually not fatal.

BABY NILE MONITOR
▼

How do you tell the difference between male and female lizards?

In some species of lizards, males may be more colorful or larger than the females. In other species, such as geckos, males may have larger tails than females. Male lizards have hemi-penes located in the **anal plate** which is used for mating.

by Pat Turcott

23

Chapter Six

Self-Defense

Do lizards hiss?

Are there any venomous lizards?

Read on to learn how
Beaded and Monitor Lizards defend themselves.

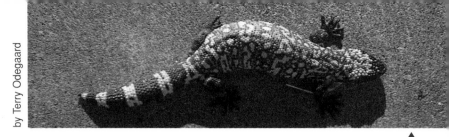

by Terry Odegaard

▲
THE GILA MONSTER IS THE ONLY POISONOUS LIZARD FOUND IN THE UNITED STATES.

Do Monitors and Beaded Lizards make themselves bigger?

Yes. The Australian Perentie Monitor often puffs out its neck and fills its body with air for protection. When this happens, it looks twice its size.

Do lizards hiss?

Yes. Gila Monsters and Mexican Beaded Lizards will often hiss when frightened. The Gila Monster will open its mouth, wave its head back and forth and wiggle its tail.

Are there any venomous lizards?

Yes. There are two species: the Gila Monster from the southwestern United States and the Mexican Beaded Lizard from Mexico and parts of Central America.

Are lizard's legs powerful?

Some species of lizards, such as the Lace Monitor from Australia, have very powerful legs to help them catch food and run away from their enemies.

by Terry Odegaard

▲
THE MEXICAN BEADED LIZARD IS THE LARGEST VENOMOUS LIZARD, BUT SHARES THE SAME HABITS AS ITS COUSIN, THE GILA MONSTER.

Why does a lizard have scales?

Different species of lizards have different types of scales. Green Tree Monitors have smooth scales which are used to keep them on their toes. Beaded Lizards have large rough scales which are used for protection against enemies.

25

Chapter Seven

Facts about Beaded and Monitor Lizards

Lizards can be our friends. They eat harmful insects that destroy our crops. If one lives on your fence, do not bother it and it will not bother you.

What can you do to protect lizards?

This is one of the many questions you will find in this chapter.

Why are some lizards so very rare?

Many species, such as the Desert Monitor, are very rare because of habitat destruction. Other species of lizards are losing their homes because the rain forest is being cut down. We should protect all species of lizards and animals in all areas.

y Wildlife World Zoo

ENDANGERED

What does endangered species mean?

The word *endangered* means a species threatened with extinction. Every day a number of species of animals becomes endangered or even becomes extinct.

◀ BENGAL MONITORS ARE ENDANGERED SPECIES.

Why are some lizards hunted and killed?

Some species of lizards are very popular on the pet trade and are often captured for this reason. Some species are killed for no reason at all.

◀ THE RED TEGU IS VERY POPULAR WITH COLLECTORS AND SHOULD HAVE LAWS TO PROTECT THEM IN THEIR WILD STATE.

by Terry Odegaard

What can I do to protect lizards?

The best thing to do to protect lizards is to pick up litter and throw it in a garbage receptacle, and leave them alone. You should learn more about the lizards in your area so you can help protect them. It is very reward-ing when you do this and it makes you feel good.

THE LAKE HABITAT IS HOME FOR MANY SPECIES OF MONITORS. THE BEST THING YOU CAN DO TO HELP LIZARDS IS TO MAKE SURE THEIR HOME IS KEPT FREE FROM POLLUTION.
▼

by Terry Odegaard

If I want to be a scientist and study lizards, what will I be?

If you want to study lizards when you grow up, you can become a *herpetologist*. Many herpetologists spend their whole lives trying to protect and conserve different species of lizards.

Do Monitor Lizards have any cousins?

Yes. Although the Tuatara (To-A-Tar-A) is not in the Monitor family, they are closely related. A Tuatara is a large spiny quadruped reptile located on islands off the coast of New Zealand. It is the only surviving *Rhynchocephalian* order. It was given a German name meaning bridge lizard in 1868 by the most famous Berlin zoologist, E. Von Martens. The name Tuatara is from the Moasis natives of New Zealand and means spine bearer.

ACCORDING TO SCIENTISTS, THE TUATARA SEEMS TO THRIVE IN COOLER TEMPERATURES UNLIKE ITS OTHER REPTILIAN COUSINS.

St. Louis Zoo

What does the word saurian mean?

The word saurian means any of a group of reptiles including lizards, and in older classifications crocodiles, and other various extinct forms which have the characteristics of lizards.

Is there such a thing as a living fossil?

A sphenodon, known as a Tuatara, is found on a few small islands of New Zealand and is a living *fossil*. Scientists have found relatives of these ancient reptiles from the Triassic period about 200 million years ago.

29

Glossary

Anal Plate:
The large scale between the back legs of the lizard.

Chlamydosaurus King II:
A scientific name for frilled lizard.

Cold-Blooded:
Having a body temperature not internally regulated, but approximately that of the environment.

Endangered: Threatened with extinction.

Endemic:
Native to a particular country, nation or region.

External:
Having merely the outward appearance of something.

Fossil:
A remnant impression, or trace of an animal or plant of past geological ages that has been preserved in the earth's crust.

Herpetologist:
One who studies reptiles and amphibians.

Neonate: Newborn.

Paleontologist:
One who studies the science dealing with the life of past geological periods as known from fossil remains.

Parasite:
An organism that lives in or on another organism at whose expense it receives nourishment.

Poacher:
One who kills or takes game and fish illegally.

Quadrupole:
A system composed of two dipoles of equal but oppositely directed moment.

Rhynchocephalian:
A class of reptile.

Scientist:
A scientific investigator.

Unisexual:
All individuals are females that can lay eggs and are fertile without mating.

Virus:
The causative agent of an infectious disease.

Warm-Blooded:
Having a relatively high and constant body temperature relatively independent of the surroundings.

Books and CD-Roms Written by the Author Suggested Reading

Snakes and Other Reptiles of the Southwest

Erik D. Stoops & Annette T. Wright. 1991. Golden West Publishing Company, Phoenix, Arizona. Scientific Field Guide.

Snakes

Erik D. Stoops & Annette T. Wright. 1992. Hardback and Paperback. Sterling Publishing Company, New York. Children's non-fiction, full-color, question and answer format. First Book in Children's Nature Library Series.

Breeding Boas and Pythons

Erik D. Stoops & Annette T. Wright. 1993. TFH Publishing Company, New York. Scientific Care and Breeding Guide.

Sharks

Erik D. Stoops & Sherrie L. Stoops. Illustrated by Jeffrey L. Martin. June, 1994. Hardback and Paperback. Sterling Publishing Company, New York. Children's non-fiction, full-color, question and answer format. Second Book in Children's Nature Library Series.

Dolphins

Erik D. Stoops, Jeffrey L. Martin & Debbie L. Stone. Release date, January, 1995. Hardback and Paperback. Sterling Publishing Company, New York. Children's non-fiction, full-color, question and answer format. Third Book in Children's Nature Library Series.

Whales

Erik D. Stoops, Jeffrey L. Martin & Debbie L. Stone. Release date, March, 1995. Hardback and Paperback. Sterling Publishing Company, New York. Children's non-fiction, full-color, question and answer format. Fourth Book in Children's Nature Library Series.

Scorpions and Other Venomous Insects of the Desert

Erik D. Stoops & Jeffrey L. Martin. Release date, June, 1995. Golden West Publishing Company, Phoenix, Arizona. A user-friendly guide.

Alligators and Crocodiles

Erik D. Stoops & Debbie L. Stone. Release date, October, 1994. Sterling Publishing Company, New York. Children's non-fiction, full-color, question and answer format. Fifth Book in Children's Nature Library Series.

Wolves

Erik D. Stoops & Dagmar Fertl. Release date, December, 1996. Sterling Publishing Company, New York. Children's non-fiction, full-color, question and answer format. Sixth Book in Children's Nature Library Series.

Internet Sites:

Zoo Net:
http://www.mindspring.com/~zoonet

Herp Link:
http://home.ptd.net/~herplink/index.html

Erik Stoops:
http://www.primenet.com/~dink

Look for the Adventures of Dink the Skink Children's book series and animated CD Rom Stories coming out in 1997.

INDEX

WE WOULD LIKE TO THANK THE FOLLOWING PEOPLE FOR THEIR ENCOURAGEMENT AND PARTICIPATION:
NATIONAL ZOOLOGICAL PARK, OFFICE OF PUBLIC AFFAIRS, SUSAN BIGGS, SMITHSONIAN INSTITUTION, TERRY CHRISTOPHER, TERRY ODEGAARD, CINCINNATI ZOO AND BOTANICAL GARDENS, ST. LOUIS ZOO, BILL LUBACK'S REPTILES, INC., AMANDA JAKSHA, JESSIE COHEN, PAT TURCOTT, RODNEY FREEMAN, DIANE E. FREEMAN, STEVEN CASTANEDA, CLYDE PEELINGS OF REPTILELAND, MICKEY OLSEN OF WILDLIFE WORLD ZOO, SCOTTSDALE CHILDREN'S NATURE CENTER, DR. JEAN ARNOLD, ARIZONA GAME AND FISH DEPARTMENT, ERIN DEAN OF THE UNITED STATES FISH AND WILDLIFE SERVICE, BOB FAULKNER, DAVE PFEIFFER OF EDUCATION ON WHEELS FOR MAKING THIS PROJECT A REALITY, DR. MARTY FELDMAN, SHERRIE STOOPS, ALESHA STOOPS, VICTORIA AND JESSICA EMERY.